Artificial Intelligence

"Navigating The Future of Business and Society."

BY: Anthony A. O'Brien

FORWARD

In my view, success isn't about pretending you have all the answers. It's about being willing to face your weaknesses and, more importantly, protect your ego. As business owners, we have plenty to be egotistical about; we've invested more, grown faster, and developed better technology than the competition. But if we don't acknowledge where we're weak, especially on something as significant as Artificial Intelligence, we're just setting ourselves up to lose.

I'm not a technical person, and I don't want to be one. I've always believed that if you want to achieve what others don't, you have to be willing to do what others won't. For most of us, *"doing the work"* on AI feels like trying to learn a new language while the floor is on fire. It's tempting to just outsource the whole process; to hand off your success to someone else and hope they get the inputs right. But you can't control your outcomes if you don't manage the inputs. That's why I'm so excited about this book.

Anthony O'Brien has done what most *"tech gurus"* aren't willing to do: he's made it practical and actionable. He understands that even if we excel at what we do, AI is an area where we likely have gaps. Anthony helps us bridge those gaps with maximum effort and focus. He's not here to teach you how to code; he's here to show you how to take a big swing. He knows that when you combine rapid experimentation with disciplined controls, you don't just see linear growth, you experience exponential growth. In business, we're bound to make some mistakes. We'll lose a few battles. But as I always tell my team, failure is simply a stepping stone toward success. It's completely within our control how we respond and how we use tools like AI to improve our talent, management, and processes. Anthony provides the roadmap for the next chapter of this journey. Tony takes AI from an uncertain *"maybe"* to an empowering reality for 2026 and beyond. This isn't just a book to be proud of; it's a resource filled with tremendous upside potential for anyone ready to put in the work.

Jordan Lee
Founder & CEO
AI Acquisition

DEDICATION

To my dearest Madison,

You are the love of my life, my unwavering support, and my best friend. Your presence fills my days with joy and purpose.

Your dedication and energy inspire me to be my best self every day. Together, we are unstoppable, moving forward hand in hand.

Thank you for your unwavering support in this latest endeavor.

PREFACE

Artificial Intelligence (AI) is a strategic technology that merges advances in computer science, engineering, cognitive science, and data disciplines to automate decision-making, generate actionable insights, and enhance customer and operational outcomes. For executives, AI is less an academic pursuit and more a capability that transforms processes, reduces costs, accelerates innovation, and creates new revenue streams.

Because AI draws from multiple fields, data engineering, machine learning, human factors, and domain expertise, successful adoption requires cross-functional alignment: clear business objectives, high-quality data, robust infrastructure, and governance to manage risk and compliance. This guide focuses on practical implications for leaders: how to prioritize high-value use cases, build the organizational and technical foundations, manage change, and measure ROI.

Read on for a pragmatic roadmap that translates AI's technical promise into measurable business results and repeatable practices you can deploy across your organization.

Historical Context and Development

From a business perspective, AI's evolution since the mid-20th century, from Alan Turing's foundational concepts through symbolic AI, statistical machine learning, and today's deep learning, represents a series of capability inflection points that have expanded what companies can automate and monetize. Each stage changed the commercial playbook: symbolic systems enabled rule-based automation for predictable processes; machine learning introduced data-driven optimization for forecasting and decisioning; deep learning unlocked scalable perception and natural-language applications that improve customer engagement and operational efficiency. For leaders, this history highlights practical lessons: match the technology to the use case, invest in data and infrastructure early, build appropriate talent and governance, and plan investments with realistic timelines informed by past cycles of hype and consolidation.

Main Areas of AI

1. **Machine Learning (ML)**
    - Enables systems to learn patterns from data and improve performance without explicit rules.

- Includes supervised, unsupervised, and reinforcement learning; common methods include decision trees, ensemble methods, and neural networks.
- Example: Recommendation systems and fraud detection.

2. **Deep Learning**
   - A subfield of ML that uses multi-layer neural networks to learn hierarchical representations from large datasets.
   - Powers state-of-the-art results in perception and language tasks.
   - Example: Image classifiers, large language models.
3. **Reinforcement Learning (RL)**
   - Learns decision-making policies by trial and error to maximize cumulative reward, often in sequential environments.
   - Used for game playing, robotics control, and resource allocation.
   - Example: Autonomous agents that learn to navigate or play coplex games.
4. **Natural Language Processing (NLP)**
   - Enables machines to understand, generate, and interact using human language.
   - Tasks include translation, summarization, sentiment analysis, question answering, and dialogue.
   - Example: Chatbots (Don't delete Chatbots) and machine translation.

5. **Computer Vision**
    - Teaches machines to interpret visual information from images or video.
    - Tasks include classification, object detection, segmentation, and 3D perception.
    - Example: Medical (Don't delete Medical) image analysis and autonomous driving perception.
6. **Robotics and Embodied AI**
    - Combines AI with mechanical systems for perception, planning, control, and manipulation in the physical world.
    - Challenges include real-time sensing, motion planning, and robust control.
    - Example: warehouse robots and service robots.
7. **Speech and Audio Processing**
    - Covers speech recognition, speech synthesis (text-to-speech), speaker identification, and audio event detection.
    - Example: Virtual assistants and automated captioning.
8. **Knowledge Representation & Reasoning**
    - Focuses on how to represent structured knowledge (ontologies, knowledge graphs) and perform logical or probabilistic inference.
    - Useful for explainable decision-making and complex query answering.
    - Example: Semantic search and expert systems.

9. **Planning, Scheduling & Optimization**
    - Involves algorithms to generate action sequences or resource allocations that satisfy constraints and optimize objectives.
    - Techniques include classical planning, motion planning, and combinatorial optimization.
10. **Multi-Agent System**
    - Studies interactions among multiple autonomous agents, including cooperation, competition, and communication.
    - Applies game theory, distributed learning, and coordination algorithms.
    - Example: Traffic signal coordination and multi-robot teams.
11. **Human-AI Interaction, Interpretability & Ethics**
    - Covers explainability, human-centered design, bias mitigation, privacy, and regulation.
    - Focuses on making AI systems usable, understandable, fair, and safe for humans.
    - Example: Tools that explain model decisions and auditing pipelines for fairness.

AI's Applications

AI is used in many fields by training computer models on data to do specific jobs.

In **Healthcare**, AI can read medical images and records to help diagnose disease, estimate patient risk, and predict how a treatment will work; these tools are checked for accuracy and must be carefully tested before clinical use.

In **Finance**, AI helps decide credit, spot fraud, and run trading strategies; success is measured by financial returns and how well problems are detected, often tested on historical data.

In **Education**, AI systems track student progress and adapt lessons to each learner; improved test scores and learning outcomes judge their value.

In **Entertainment**, recommendation systems and generative models suggest or create content; they're evaluated by user engagement (clicks, watch time) and human judgments of quality.

Across all areas, reliable AI depends on good data, models that work on new situations, explainability, privacy protections, and rules to reduce bias and keep systems safe.

Ethical Issues and the Future For Business Leaders

Context and Opportunity

AI is driving material value across industries (revenue growth, cost reduction, customer personalization, operational efficiency). At the same time, its rapid progress creates ethical, legal, reputational, and operational risks that can materially affect business outcomes. Responsible AI is not only a compliance requirement, but it is also a strategic differentiator. Companies that embed ethics, robustness, and transparency into AI product lifecycles reduce downside risk and unlock greater trust, adoption, and long-term value.

Top Ethical and Strategic Risks to the Business

- **Privacy And Data Breaches:** Unauthorized use or leakage of sensitive data can lead to regulatory fines and loss of customer trust.
- **Bias And Discrimination:** Models trained on biased data can produce unfair outcomes, exposing the company to legal, reputational, and customer retention risks.
- **Lack Of Transparency And Explainability:** Opaque decisions in high-stakes contexts (finance, healthcare, HR) can block adoption and invite regulatory scrutiny.
- **Safety And Robustness Failures:** Model errors under distribution shift, adversarial inputs, or system failures can cause operational disruption and liability.

- **Regulatory And Compliance Risk:** Emerging AI-specific regulation (data protection, automated decision rules, sectoral requirements) increases compliance complexity.
- **Workforce And Business Model Disruption:** Automation impacts jobs and requires reskilling and organizational change management.
- **Concentration And Vendor Risk:** Reliance on third-party models or cloud providers creates supply-chain and concentration risks.

Strategic Priorities (What Leaders Should Focus On)

1. **Governance And Accountability**
    - Put AI risk on the enterprise risk register. Assign clear ownership (board oversight + executive sponsor).
    - Establish an AI governance body (cross-functional: legal, privacy, security, product, HR, compliance, domain experts).
2. **Risk-Proportionate Controls**
    - Classify AI use cases by risk (low, medium, high) and apply controls appropriate to risk level (lighter for personalization, stringent for high-stakes decisions).
    - Require pre-deployment impact assessments for medium/high-risk applications.

3. **Data And Privacy Practices**
    - Enforce data minimization, access controls, and provenance tracking.
    - Adopt privacy-preserving techniques (anonymization standards, differential privacy, federated learning where appropriate).
4. **Fairness, Transparency, And Explainability**
    - Integrate fairness checks into model development; measure subgroup performance and disparate impact.
    - Publish model documentation (model cards, data sheets) and provide stakeholder-appropriate explanations for decisions.
5. **Robustness And Monitoring**
    - Build automated monitoring for model drift, performance degradation, and adversarial behavior.
    - Implement incident response procedures and rollback capability.
6. **People And Change Management**
    - Invest in reskilling and redeployment programs.
    - Define human-in-the-loop rules for high-stakes decisions and ensure clear escalation pathways.
7. **Vendor And Third-Party Risk Management**
    - Require transparency from suppliers, data provenance guarantees, and contractual SLAs for model behavior, updates, and security.

8. **Environmental And Ethical Footprint**
    - Track and reduce the carbon footprint of model training and inference; include sustainability in procurement decisions.
9. **Immediate Actions (0–6 Months)**
    - Conduct an AI inventory and risk classification across products and internal tools.
    - Run a targeted AI impact assessment for the top 3 high-risk use cases.
    - Appoint an AI ethical lead or committee and add AI to the board-level agenda.
    - Implement basic monitoring and logging for deployed models; enforce access controls on datasets.
    - Create a vendor due diligence checklist for third-party AI providers.
10. **Mid-Term Actions (6–24 Months)**
    - Standardize development pipelines with built-in fairness tests, explainability checks, and privacy controls.
    - Establish regular independent audits and red-team exercises for high-risk systems.
    - Integrate AI KPIs into business dashboards (see KPIs below).
    - Launch workforce reskilling programs aligned to strategic priorities.

11. Long-Term Preparedness (24+ Months)

- Invest in research partnerships and participation in industry standards/consortia.
- Build internal capability for validating advanced models and for evaluating emerging governance/regulatory frameworks.
- Maintain scenario planning for systemic risks (large-scale failures, misuse, and advanced capability developments).

12. Key KPIs And Metrics To Track

- Business impact: revenue lift, cost savings, conversion/engagement uplift attributable to AI.
- Risk metrics: number of high-risk deployments, incidents per quarter, mean time to detection/mitigation.
- Model performance: accuracy/recall/AUC by subgroup, drift rate, uptime.
- Compliance metrics: results of audits, percentage of systems with documented impact assessments.
- People metrics: percentage of workforce reskilled, employee satisfaction in impacted roles.
- Sustainability: energy per model-training job, carbon emissions linked to compute.

13. Board-Level Asks (What You Can Authorize Now)

- Approve budget for an 8-12-week AI readiness assessment (inventory, risk classification, roadmap).

- Mandate quarterly AI risk reporting to the board and create an AI oversight committee.
- Allocate funds for prioritized controls: monitoring tooling, privacy solutions, auditing, and workforce retraining.

14. Business Case Framing

- Responsible AI reduces tail risk (legal, reputational, operational) and increases commercial adoption and customer trust.
- Upfront investment in governance and tooling lowers expected loss from incidents and enables faster, safer scaling of AI capabilities.

15. Next Step (Recommended)

- Commission an 8-week AI readiness & risk assessment that delivers: AI inventory, top 3 prioritized risks/opportunities, remediation roadmap, and estimated budget/timeline for implementation.

Contents

INTRODUCTION

Artificial Intelligence is no longer a speculative technology; it is a strategic capability that directly influences revenue, costs, customer experience, and operational resilience. When applied to the right problems, AI enables personalized customer engagement and new product offerings, automates routine processes to reduce operating expenses, (don't delete) surfaces real-time insights for faster, better decisions, and scales scarce expertise across the enterprise.

For business leaders, extracting value from AI requires a clear, risk-aware approach: prioritize high-impact use cases tied to measurable KPIs, invest in the data and talent needed to execute, and put governance in place to manage privacy, fairness, and reliability. Organizations that pair rapid experimentation with disciplined controls capture competitive advantage more quickly while minimizing regulatory, reputational, and operational downside.

The Importance of AI in Business

Adding AI to business operations offers several strong benefits:

- **Better Decision-Making:** AI ingests streaming and historical data to deliver real-time, predictive insights and scenario simulations that shorten decision cycles and increase accuracy. By surfacing leading indicators, prioritizing opportunities, and automating routine tradeoffs with human-in-the-loop controls,

AI enables faster, more consistent strategic and operational choices, measurable through reduced time-to-decision, improved forecast accuracy, higher conversion rates, and lower operating costs. Integrate AI outputs into existing workflows and pair them with clear governance and explainability standards so leaders can act quickly and confidently.

- **Greater Operational Efficiency:** AI automates repetitive, rules-based work, such as data entry, invoice processing, and routine customer inquiries, freeing employees to focus on higher-value, strategic activities. This drives faster throughput, lower error and rework rates, and measurable cost savings while enabling scalable capacity without linear headcount growth. To capture value quickly, integrate automation into end-to-end workflows with human-in-the-loop exception handling, track baseline KPIs (cycle time, error rate, cost per transaction), and invest in reskilling and change management.
- **Customized Customer Experiences:** AI synthesizes first- and third-party signals to deliver timely, hyper-relevant recommendations and personalized messaging across channels, driving higher conversion, retention, and customer lifetime value. Use recommendation engines, propensity models, and real-time orchestration to enable dynamic offers, next-best-actions, and tailored journeys at scale, while

embedding consent management and data-minimization to protect privacy. Track impact with KPIs such as conversion uplift, average order value, repeat purchase rate, and CLTV, and operationalize by integrating models with your CRM/CDP, running A/B tests, and continuously monitoring for performance drift and fairness.

- **Enhanced Risk Management:** AI analyzes large, diverse data streams in real time to surface patterns, anomalies, and leading indicators, enabling earlier detection of fraud, credit deterioration, cyber threats, supply-chain disruptions, and compliance lapses. Coupled with scenario simulation and automated alerts plus human review, these capabilities let organizations move from reactive remediation to proactive mitigation, reducing financial loss, shortening detection-to-response times, and improving capital and reserve allocation. To capture value, embed AI into existing risk frameworks, define clear escalation and governance rules, and monitor key metrics such as detection lead time, true/false-positive rates, and loss prevented, while regularly validating models for robustness and fairness.

The Value of This Book

This book is written for business leaders and practitioners who must turn AI from a technical buzzword into a measurable business impact. It delivers a practical, action-oriented roadmap to select, implement, and govern AI initiatives that drive revenue, reduce cost, and de-risk operations.

What you'll get:

- **Executive Primer:** Concise, non-technical explanations of core AI concepts so decision-makers can evaluate opportunities and tradeoffs quickly.
- **Business Cases And Metrics:** Industry-relevant examples that tie AI solutions to KPIs (revenue lift, cost per transaction, time-to-insight, CLTV, loss prevented) and templates to quantify ROI.
- **Implementation Playbook:** Step-by-step guidance on scoping pilots, building data and model capabilities, integrating AI into workflows, and scaling successful projects.
- **Risk And Governance Framework:** Practical controls for privacy, compliance, model validation, and human-in-the-loop processes to manage operational and reputational risk.
- **Organizational Adoption:** Strategies for change management, reskilling, vendor selection, and aligning incentives to capture value at scale.

How to use it:

- Apply the playbook to run fast experiments and measure outcomes against clear KPIs.
- Start with the readiness checklist to prioritize 1–2 high-impact, low-risk pilots.
- Use the governance guidance to institutionalize safe, repeatable AI practices as you scale.
- Outcome: A pragmatic, repeatable approach that helps your organization move from AI experimentation to a consistent, measurable business advantage.

Chapter 1

What Is Artificial Intelligence?

Artificial Intelligence (AI) enables computers to perform tasks that normally require human judgment, learning from data, recognizing patterns, making predictions, and understanding language and images. For business leaders, AI is a practical toolkit for automating routine work, augmenting decision-making with predictive insights, personalizing customer experiences at scale, and improving operational efficiency.

Coined in 1956 by John McCarthy as *"the science and engineering of making intelligent machines,"* AI has moved from academic theory to a suite of deployable technologies (machine learning, natural language processing, computer vision) that convert data into measurable business outcomes. Successful adoption depends on clear objectives, quality data, and governance to capture value reliably and responsibly.

Defining Artificial Intelligence

Artificial Intelligence (AI) is a portfolio of technologies that enable machines to perform tasks that traditionally require human cognition, learning from data, recognizing patterns, making predictions, understanding language, and interpreting images. For business leaders, AI is less about the underlying algorithms and more about the capabilities and outcomes it unlocks: faster insights, automated decisioning, personalized customer engagement, and predictive risk detection.

Key Components (What AI Does)

- **Predict And Recommend:** Forecast demand, recommend products, score credit risk.
- **Automate Routine Work:** Process invoices, route claims, and handle common customer inquiries.
- **Interpret Unstructured Data:** Analyze text, speech, and images to extract actionable signals.
- **Optimize Decisions:** Improve pricing, inventory, and operations through continuous feedback.

Common technologies

- Machine learning and deep learning, natural language processing, computer vision, reinforcement learning, and robotic process automation.

What matters for business success

- Clear business objectives and KPIs, high-quality data, integration into workflows, measurable pilots, and governance (privacy, fairness, model validation).
- Start with small, outcome-driven experiments, measure ROI, then scale with controls and change management.
- In short: AI is a practical toolkit for converting data into repeatable business advantage when applied with clear goals, data discipline, and governance.

Historical Context

AI has progressed from theoretical research to a producible, scalable capability. Its history explains why current opportunities are practical and wide-ranging, and why successful adoption requires investment in data, compute, integration, and governance.

The history of AI begins in the mid-20th century, marked by important milestones:

- **1940s-1950s:** Foundational computing research established the idea that machines could perform cognitive tasks. Alan Turing's 1950 framing of machine intelligence introduced the core business question: which human decisions can be automated or augmented?
- **1956 (Dartmouth):** Formal birth of AI as a research field. That institutional focus set the stage for sustained investment in automation and decision-support technologies.
- **1980s-1990s:** Advances in machine learning and neural networks enabled systems to learn from data rather than relying solely on rules. For business, this unlocked practical capabilities in pattern recognition, early speech recognition, and predictive analytics
- **2000s-present:** The combination of large datasets, cheaper compute, deep learning breakthroughs, cloud infrastructure, and open-source tools turned AI into deployable products, natural language processing, computer vision, recommendation engines, and autonomous systems. This period shifted AI from experimental labs to enterprise scale, lowering adoption costs and increasing measurable impact across functions (marketing, operations, risk, R&D).

Key Components of AI

AI comprises several core capabilities that translate directly into commercial value. Below are the components executives should understand, with concise business definitions and real-world examples showing measurable impact.

1. **Learning**
   - **Business Definition:** Systems that improve performance over time by analyzing data and adapting models to drive better outcomes.
   - **Example:** Agricultural platforms that analyze weather and soil data to optimize planting schedules.
   - **Business Impact:** Higher yields, reduced input costs, and improved forecasting accuracy.
2. **Reasoning**
   - **Business Definition:** Algorithms that synthesize available information to draw conclusions and make decisions under uncertainty.
   - **Example:** Credit-scoring models that assess borrower risk and recommend loan approvals.
   - **Business Impact:** Faster underwriting, lower default rates, and scalable decisioning.
3. **Problem-Solving**
   - **Business Definition:** Systems that design and execute strategies to achieve specific operational objectives.
   - **Example:** Manufacturing automation that reallocates tasks between robots and humans to meet throughput targets.

- **Business Impact:** Increased productivity, lower cycle times, and redeployment of skilled labor to higher-value work.

4. **Perception**
    - **Business Definition:** Technologies that interpret sensory inputs (images, audio, video) into actionable insights.
    - **Example:** Medical imaging tools that flag anomalies for faster diagnosis.
    - **Business Impact:** Improved diagnostic speed and accuracy, reduced costs from earlier interventions.
5. **Language Understanding**
    - **Business Definition:** Capabilities to comprehend, generate, and act on human language for customer and employee interactions.
    - **Example:** AI chatbots that handle routine customer service inquiries.
    - **Business Impact:** Reduced response times, lower servicing costs, and improved customer satisfaction.

Together, these components form the foundation for industry use cases, customer experience, risk management, operations optimization, and new product creation, making AI a core enabler of cost reduction, revenue growth, and competitive differentiation.

Applications of AI

AI tools are used in many areas of daily life and industries, including:

1. **Healthcare**
    - **Business Impact:** Improves diagnostic accuracy, enables personalized treatment plans, and optimizes care management to reduce costs and readmissions.
    - **AI Capabilities:** Medical imaging analysis, predictive risk scoring, clinical decision support, NLP for records.
    - **Example:** IBM Watson Health, used to analyze large data sets to inform oncology treatment options (illustrative of decision-support deployment).
    - **Kpis To Track:** diagnostic accuracy, time-to-diagnosis, readmission rate, cost-per-case, clinician adoption.
2. **Finance**
    - **Business Impact:** Reduces fraud losses, improves credit and market risk assessment, and automates trading and back-office processes to lower operating costs.
    - **AI Capabilities:** Anomaly detection, credit scoring models, algorithmic trading, automated compliance monitoring.
    - **Example:** JPMorgan Chase's LOXM, an autonomous trading system that optimizes execution and adapts to market conditions.

- **Business Impact:** Raises learning outcomes and retention by tailoring instruction, while reducing instructor workload and scaling services
- **AI Capabilities:** Adaptive learning engines, automated assessment, intelligent tutoring systems.
- **Example:** Adaptive platforms that analyze student performance to create individualized learning paths.
- **Kpis To Track:** Learning-gain scores, course completion rates, time-to-proficiency, cost-per-learner

3. **Transportation**
   - **Business Impact:** Improves safety, reduces operating costs, and increases route efficiency and asset utilization.
   - **AI Capabilities:** Autonomous navigation, predictive maintenance, demand forecasting, dynamic routing.
   - **Example:** Waymo's self-driving taxis, an example of AI handling complex urban driving scenarios.
   - **Kpis To Track:** incidents per million miles, on-time performance, cost per mile, downtime from maintenance.
4. **Entertainment & Media**
   - **Business Impact:** Increases user engagement, retention, and monetization through personalized content and targeted recommendations.
   - **AI Capabilities:** Recommendation engines, content tagging, audience segmentation, automated content creation.

- **Example:** Streaming services (e.g., Netflix) that apply viewing data to recommend content and optimize catalogs.
- **KPIs To Track:** watch time, retention/churn rate, click-through and conversion rates, ARPU.
- **Cross-Industry Takeaway:** AI delivers value through prediction, personalization, automation, and interpretation of unstructured data.
- **For Business Leaders:** Define specific KPIs, pilot with measurable results, and scale successful models while ensuring governance and integration into core workflows.

The Evolution of AI - A Business Perspective

Overview of AI has evolved through distinct technical stages. Each stage altered what organizations could automate, the investments needed, and the business models that emerged. Understanding these phases helps leaders select the right use cases, investments, and governance for their organization.

Phases, business impact, and practical considerations;

1. **Symbolic AI (rules and logic)**
   - **What It Is:** Rule-based systems and expert systems that encode human knowledge as if-then rules and decision trees.
   - Business Impact: Delivered deterministic, auditable decision logic for constrained domains (e.g., loan approval

rules, diagnostic checklists). Useful where rules are stable and explainability is required.

- Strengths: Interpretable, low data needs, predictable behavior.
- Limitations: Brittle, hard to scale or adapt to variation, expensive to maintain as rules grow.
- When To Use: Regulatory or safety-critical workflows where traceability and control matter.
- KPIs: Rule coverage, exception rate, compliance incidents.

2. **Machine Learning (statistical models)**
   - **What It Is:** Algorithms that learn patterns from historical, labeled data (regression, trees, SVMs).
   - Business Impact: Made predictive analytics operational, customer churn models, fraud detection, and demand forecasting, enabling data-driven decisions and automation.
   - Strengths: Better generalization than rules, more flexible, widely applicable across functions.
   - Limitations: Requires labeled data and feature engineering; models can degrade if data shifts.
   - When to use: Well-instrumented processes with historical outcomes you can predict.
   - KPIs: Prediction accuracy, precision/recall, lift vs. baseline, model drift.

3. **Deep Learning (representation learning)**
    - **What It Is**: Multi-layer neural networks that learn hierarchical features from large, often unstructured datasets (images, text, audio).
    - Business Impact: Enabled high-performance perception and natural language capabilities, image analysis, speech recognition, language understanding, opening new products (chatbots, recommendation engines, automated inspection).
4. **Foundation Models and Transfer Learning (recent)**
    - **What It Is**: Large pre-trained models (language, vision, or multimodal) that can be fine-tuned or prompted for many downstream tasks.
    - Business Impact: Lowers cost and time to deploy sophisticated capabilities (summarization, semantic search, code generation), enabling rapid prototyping and product differentiation.
    - Strengths: Rapid adaptability, fewer labeled examples required, rich capabilities across tasks.
    - Limitations: Governance, data-privacy concerns, hallucination/incorrect outputs, compute and licensing costs.
    - Infrastructure: Plan for storage, compute (GPU/TPU or cloud), and MLOps for repeatable deployment.

- Governance & Risk: Implement model validation, monitoring for drift, privacy controls, and explainability where required.
- Integration: Embed models into workflows and systems, not standalone experiments, so outcomes affect KPIs.
- Economics: Measure ROI, total cost of ownership (data, compute, maintenance), and expected time to value.
- Business Leaders' Takeaway: AI has evolved from rigid rules to flexible, high-performance models. Each step broadened the range of automatable problems but raised new requirements for data, compute, and governance. Choose the approach that matches the problem's complexity, data maturity, and regulatory needs; start with focused pilots that measure business KPIs and scale with disciplined MLOps and oversight.

Ethical Considerations

As AI embeds into products and operations, ethical issues become material business risks that affect trust, compliance, brand value, and legal exposure. Below are the core areas leaders should prioritize, with examples, concrete controls, and metrics.

1. **Bias & fairness**
   - Business Risk: Discriminatory outcomes can produce legal liability, reputational damage, and poor customer outcomes.
   - Example: Hiring algorithms that unintentionally disadvantage candidates by gender, race, or age.
   - Recommended Controls: Perform bias impact assessments, use diverse training data, implement fairness-aware model design, and include humans-in-the-loop for high-stakes decisions.
   - Metrics To Monitor: Disparate impact ratios, demographic parity, complaint rate, and audit frequency.
2. **Transparency & explainability**
   - Business Risk: Opaque models reduce customer and regulator trust and hinder error resolution.
   - Example: Credit-scoring systems that customers or regulators cannot interpret.
   - Recommended Controls: Document model purpose and data lineage, provide business-level explanations for decisions, maintain model cards and decision logs, and tier explainability by risk level.
   - Metrics To Monitor: Percent of high-risk models with explainability artifacts, time to provide explanation on request, and number of interpretability incidents.

3. **Accountability & governance**
   - Business Risk: Unclear ownership for AI actions complicates incident response, insurance, and regulatory compliance.
   - Example: Liability disputes after an accident involving an autonomous vehicle.
   - Recommended Controls: Assign clear ownership (product, legal, risk), maintain incident escalation paths, require pre-deployment sign-offs, and include AI risk in board reporting.
   - Metrics To Monitor: Incident response time, number of models with assigned owners, audit and approval rates.
4. **Privacy & data protection**
   - Business Risk: Mishandling personal data can trigger fines, class actions, and customer churn.
   - Example: Patient data exposure in healthcare models violating privacy laws.
   - Recommended Controls: Minimize data collection, anonymize/pseudonymize, apply purpose limitation, enforce access controls, and embed privacy reviews into development.
   - Metrics To Monitor: Data access violations, proportion of datasets anonymized, time to remediate breaches, and privacy-impact assessment completion.

5. **Governance action items for leaders**
    - Establish an AI governance framework with cross-functional sponsorship (legal, compliance, engineering, product, ethics).
    - Require pre-deployment risk and impact assessments for high-risk systems.
    - Monitor models in production for drift, fairness, and safety; schedule regular audits.
    - Communicate transparently with customers and regulators; maintain clear policies for redress and human review.
    - Invest in training for product, risk, and compliance teams so ethical controls are operationalized.
    - Leader Takeaway: Ethical AI is not a separate compliance exercise; it's a business discipline that reduces risk and preserves trust. Build proportionate controls, measure them, and make AI ethics part of the product lifecycle and board oversight.

Distinguishing Between Narrow and General AI

Why this distinction matters: business investments, risk management, and strategic planning depend on whether the AI capability you're buying or building is task-specific (practical today) or an aspirational, general intelligence (theoretical). Treat them differently.

1. **Narrow AI (Artificial Narrow Intelligence - ANI)**
    - **What It Is**: Systems designed to perform a defined task or a limited set of tasks, often extremely well, but only within that scope.
    - Examples: Recommendation engines, fraud-detection models, voice assistants (Siri/Alexa), image recognition, chatbots for customer service, predictive maintenance. Modern large models (LLMs) are powerful but still narrow when applied to specific tasks.

    Business Implications

    - Leader Actions: Prioritize ANI projects by clear business value, ensure data readiness, implement MLOps and monitoring, and apply proportionate governance.
    - Immediate ROI Potential: Use cases are well understood and can be measured against KPIs.
    - Faster Deployment: Predictable project scope, existing vendor solutions, cloud infrastructure, and mature MLOps practices.
    - Manageable Risk Profile: Risks are operational (bias, drift, privacy) and governed by standard controls.
2. **General AI (Artificial General Intelligence - AGI)**
    - **What It Is:** A hypothetical system with human-level or broader general intelligence that can understand, learn, and apply knowledge across arbitrary tasks and domains.

- Key Characteristics (if realized): broad transfer learning, flexible reasoning, autonomous problem solving across contexts.
- Current Status: Largely theoretical, no consensus that AGI exists or on a reliable timeline. Most current breakthroughs advance narrow capabilities rather than genuine general intelligence.

Business Implications

- Leader Actions: Monitor research and policy developments, avoid diverting core resources to speculative AGI projects, but include scenario planning and strategic watch functions.
- Speculative Strategic Bets: AGI would reshape business models and risk frameworks, but it remains uncertain when or if it will arrive.
- Different Governance Needs: Would require new legal, ethical, and safety frameworks beyond current compliance practices.

Practical Guidance For Leaders

- Prioritize narrow, measurable use cases with clear KPIs and data readiness.
- Invest in infrastructure, MLOps, talent, and governance that scale across multiple ANI projects.

- Maintain an R&D or strategic watch team to track AGI research, regulation, and competitive moves, and use scenario planning rather than heavy investment.
- Apply Different Risk Tolerances: Operational controls for ANI deployments; strategic, cross-functional risk planning for AGI scenarios.

Quick Checklist

- Is the use case well defined and measurable? (If yes → ANI approach.)
- Do we have quality historical data and a path to integrate the model into workflows? (If yes → proceed with ANI pilot.)
- Are we funding basic research or scenario planning around general intelligence? (If yes → keep it separate and limited; treat as strategic bet.)
- Bottom line: build capabilities and controls around today's narrow AI to drive value and manage risk; keep an informed but cautious posture toward AGI.

Key Differences Between Narrow and General AI

1. **Scope and flexibility**
    - Narrow AI: Designed for specific, well-defined tasks (e.g., fraud detection, recommendation engines).

- Business Implication: Enables immediate, measurable automation and efficiency gains within confined workflows.
- Action: Prioritize narrow use cases that map directly to KPIs and are easy to integrate with existing systems.
- General AI: Hypothetical capability to perform any intellectual task a human can, across domains.
- Business Implication: Would transform strategy, products, and workforce models, but timing and feasibility are uncertain.
- Action: Treat as long-term strategic scenarios; do not base near-term operating plans on its arrival.

2. **Learning and adaptation**
   - Narrow AI: Improves within its task through focused training and retraining; does not generalize knowledge across unrelated tasks.
   - Business Implication: Continuous value requires ongoing data pipelines, monitoring for drift, and periodic model updates.
   - Action: Invest in MLOps, data quality, and change management to sustain performance and ROI.
   - General AI: Would be expected to transfer learning across contexts and learn new domains autonomously (if realized).

- Business Implication: Would reduce the need for task-specific models and reshape talent and process needs, but this remains speculative.
- Action: Monitor research and experiment selectively with transfer learning/foundation models that offer some cross-task benefits today.

3. **Current status and risk profile**
   - Narrow AI: Mature and widely deployed across industries; risks are operational (bias, privacy, model drift, explainability).
   - Business Implication: Deployments can be rapid but require governance, compliance, and clear ROI measurement.
   - Action: Implement proportionate controls: privacy safeguards, fairness testing, explainability for high-risk use cases, and KPIs for business outcomes.
   - General AI: Largely theoretical with no proven systems meeting human-level general intelligence.
   - Business Implication: Legal, ethical, and safety frameworks for AGI would be fundamentally different and require cross-sector coordination.
   - Action: Maintain strategic watch, engage in policy dialogue, and include AGI scenarios in enterprise risk planning without heavy capital diversion.

4. **Executive takeaway**
    - Narrow AI is the practical source of near-term value: focus investments on measurable, well-scoped projects with strong data and governance.
    - AGI is a speculative strategic consideration: monitor developments and prepare governance scenarios, but prioritize operationalizing ANI capabilities today.

Conclusion

Artificial Intelligence is a strategic enabler that can materially improve productivity, customer experience, and cost structures across industries. For leaders, the priority is not debating the technology in the abstract but turning AI into measurable business outcomes while managing attendant risks.

Recommended Next Steps

- **Focus On Value:** Start with well-scoped, high-ROI ANI pilots tied to clear KPIs and a plan to scale successful projects.
- **Build The Foundation:** Invest in data quality, MLOps, and interoperable infrastructure so models deliver reliable, repeatable results.
- **Govern Proportionately:** Deploy privacy, fairness, explainability, and monitoring controls appropriate to each use case's risk profile.

- **Align Talent And Partners:** Combine internal capabilities with strategic vendors to accelerate time-to-value and fill skill gaps.
- **Measure And Iterate:** Track business metrics, monitor model drift, and iterate quickly to protect and grow benefit.
- **Monitor The Horizon:** Maintain a strategic watch for research, regulation, and broader AGI-related developments; include scenario planning without diverting core resources.

Chapter 2

Historical Overview of Artificial Intelligence

Why history matters for leaders: The evolution of AI is not just a chronology of discoveries; it shows how technical breakthroughs translate into commercial opportunities, investment cycles, talent shifts, and governance needs. Understanding the milestones helps executives distinguish hype from deployable capability, plan realistic timelines, and extract organizational lessons from past cycles.

Key Milestones And Their Business Implications

1. **Philosophical Foundations (Ancient To Classical)**
    - What Happened: Early ideas about reasoning and artificial agents (from Greek myths to Aristotle's logic) set the conceptual groundwork for formal reasoning and automated decision-making.

- Business Implication: AI's roots in logic and structure explain why many enterprise applications succeed when problems are well-defined and ruleable (e.g., compliance, automated workflows).

2. **The Turing Test (1950)**
   - What Happened: Alan Turing framed a behavioral test for machine intelligence, shifting focus from how machines think to what they can do in practice.
   - Business Implication: Reinforced outcome-oriented metrics, usefulness, and user experience matter more than internal complexity. For leaders: define clear acceptance criteria for AI products, not philosophical benchmarks.
3. **Dartmouth Conference (1956)**
   - What Happened: The field of *"Artificial Intelligence"* was formally named, and a research community formed.
   - Business Implication: Demonstrates the role of academic convening in launching ecosystems. Commercialization follows community formation, invest in partnerships with research labs and universities to access early talent and ideas.
4. **The Logic Theorist (1956)**
   - What Happened: An early program that automated theorem proving, showing machines could outperform humans on specific cognitive tasks.

- Business Implication: Early proof that automation yields efficiency gains in knowledge-intensive tasks.
- Lesson: Look for high-value, repeatable cognitive tasks that can be codified and automated.

5. **The Perceptron (1958)**
   - What Happened: Early neural network architecture for pattern recognition, an initial step toward learning systems.
   - Business Implication: Signals the shift from purely rule-based automation to data-driven models.
   - For Business: Invest in data capture and labeling early; data is the raw material for future AI value.
6. **ELIZA (1966)**
   - What Happened: A simple natural language system that simulated conversation and highlighted the user's perception of *"understanding."*
   - Business Implication: User experience can drive adoption even when the underlying technology is simple. Prioritize customer-facing piloting to validate value, not perfect technical completeness.
7. **Shakey the Robot (1969)**
   - What Happened: First mobile robot integrating perception, planning, and action.
   - Business Implication: Demonstrates the complexity and integration costs of physical AI systems. For operations or

robotics investments: factor systems integration, safety, and maintenance into the total cost of ownership.

Strategic Lessons for Business Leaders

- **Value is incremental and domain specific:** Major commercial impact comes from narrow, well-scoped use cases, not from abstract claims of *"intelligence."*
- **Data Precedes Capability:** Historical advances moved from rules to learning; organizations need to prioritize data strategy (collection, quality, governance) to capture future value.
- **Ecosystems Matter:** Partnerships with academia, startups, and cloud providers accelerate access to innovation and talent.
- **Integration and Change Management Drive ROI:** Technical prototypes fail to deliver unless integrated into workflows, supported by MLOps, and accompanied by change programs.
- **Expect Cycles Of Hype And Reality:** History shows alternating optimism and setbacks, use staged investments and pilots to manage risk.
- **Bottom Line:** AI's history shows a steady progression from conceptual ideas to domain-specific, deployable systems.
- **For business leaders, the takeaway is practical:** Focus on deployable narrow AI that maps to measurable outcomes, invest in data and integration capabilities, and maintain a strategic watch for longer-term shifts.

Key Figures and Their Contributions

1. **Alan Turing**
    - Contribution: Framed the practical benchmark for machine intelligence (the Turing Test) and helped establish computing theory.
    - Business Implication: Focus on observable performance and user outcomes when evaluating AI solutions, measure impact, not just technical novelty.
2. **John McCarthy**
    - Contribution: Coined the term *"Artificial Intelligence,"* created the Lisp programming language, and helped formalize AI as a field.
    - Business Implication: Invest in the right toolchains and talent ecosystems; terminology and standards shape markets and hiring.
3. **Marvin Minsky**
    - Contribution: Advanced cognitive architectures and early thinking on how machines could model human thought.
    - Business Implication: Complex problems require architectural thinking, design AI systems with cognitive workflows and integration in mind.

4. **Allen Newell and Herbert A. Simon**
    - Contribution: Built early problem-solving programs (Logic Theorist, General Problem Solver) and advanced the study of decision processes.
    - Business Implication: Automation of repeatable cognitive tasks drives efficiency, target ruleable, high-value decision workflows first.
5. **Joseph Weizenbaum**
    - Contribution: Created ELIZA, an early natural language program that highlighted both technical capability and user perception.
    - Business Implication: User experience and perception can drive adoption; be transparent about capabilities and limits to manage expectations and reputation.
6. **Frank Rosenblatt**
    - Contribution: Introduced the perceptron, an early neural network for pattern recognition.
    - Business Implication: Signals the shift to data-driven models, prioritize data collection, labeling, and governance to realize ML value.
7. **Claude Shannon**
    - Contribution: Founded information theory and contributed to algorithmic approaches for game playing and communication.

- Business Implication: Data quality, signal processing, and efficient algorithms underpin scalable AI products, optimize data pipelines, and model efficiency

8. **William Ross Ashby**
   - Contribution: Work in cybernetics and adaptive systems, emphasizing resilience and feedback.
   - Business Implication: Design AI systems for adaptability and robust feedback loops to handle real-world variability and drift.

9. **J.C.R. Licklider**
   - Contribution: Proposed *"man-computer symbiosis,"* envisioning collaborative human-computer problem solving.
   - Business Implication: Best outcomes often come from hybrid models that combine human judgment with AI automation for higher-risk or complex decisions.
   - Business Implication: Domain expertise is a strategic asset; capture expert knowledge into systems where it yields repeatable business value.

10. **Geoffrey Hinton, Yann LeCun, Yoshua Bengio**
    - Contribution: Led the breakthroughs in deep learning that underpin many modern AI capabilities.
    - Business Implication: Deep learning drives current competitive advantage; invest in talent, compute, and data infrastructure if pursuing advanced ML use cases.

Conclusion

The history of AI highlights recurring business themes: the shift from rule-based to data-driven approaches, the critical role of data and integration, the need for human-machine collaboration, and the importance of managing expectations and ethics. Translate these lessons into strategy by prioritizing measurable, domain-specific pilots; building data and MLOps capabilities; embedding domain expertise; and designing systems for resilience and human oversight.

Chapter 3
Machine Learning

Machine Learning (ML), a branch of Artificial Intelligence (AI), enables systems to analyze data, identify patterns, and make decisions with little human input. In business, ML is transforming operations by improving decision-making, streamlining processes, and fostering innovation. This chapter covers the basics of machine learning algorithms and reviews their main applications in business: supervised, unsupervised, and reinforcement learning.

Supervised Learning in Business

Supervised learning involves training algorithms on labeled datasets to predict outcomes for new, unseen data. In business, this approach is widely used for:

- **Customer Segmentation:** Analyzing customer data to identify distinct groups, enabling targeted marketing strategies.
- **Sales Forecasting:** Predicting future sales based on historical data, aiding in inventory management and resource allocation.
- **Credit Scoring:** Assessing the creditworthiness of individuals or businesses by analyzing financial histories.

Unsupervised Learning in Business

Unsupervised learning deals with unlabeled data and uncovers hidden patterns and intrinsic structures. Its business applications include:

- **Market Basket Analysis:** Identifying product associations to optimize cross-selling and promotional strategies.
- **Anomaly Detection:** Spotting unusual patterns, such as fraudulent transactions or equipment malfunctions.
- **Customer Behavior Analysis:** Understanding purchasing behaviors to enhance product offerings and customer experiences.

Reinforcement Learning in Business

Reinforcement learning involves algorithms learning optimal behaviors through interactions with an environment, receiving feedback in the form of rewards or penalties. In business, this is applied in:

- **Dynamic Pricing:** Adjusting prices in real-time based on demand, competition, and other factors to maximize revenue.
- **Supply Chain Optimization:** Improving logistics and inventory management by learning efficient operational strategies.
- **Personalized Marketing:** Tailoring marketing efforts to individual customer preferences to increase engagement and sales.

By leveraging these machine learning techniques, businesses can gain a competitive edge, enhance operational efficiency, and deliver personalized experiences to their customers.

1. **Fundamentals of Machine Learning Algorithms**

Machine learning algorithms are designed to process and analyze large datasets, learning from them to make predictions or decisions. The fundamental steps involved in machine learning include:

- **Data Collection:** Gathering relevant and sufficient data to train the model.
- **Data Preprocessing:** Cleaning and preparing the data by handling missing values, normalizing, and encoding categorical variables.
- **Model Selection:** Choosing an appropriate algorithm based on the problem type and data characteristics.

- **Training:** Feeding the prepared data into the model to learn patterns.
- **Evaluation:** Assessing the model's performance using metrics like accuracy, precision, recall, and F1-score.
- **Deployment:** Implementing the model in a real-world environment for inference.

Standard Machine Learning Algorithms Include:

- **Linear Regression:** Models the relationship between a dependent variable and one or more independent variables.
- **Logistic Regression:** Used for binary classification tasks.
- **Decision Trees:** Model decisions and their possible consequences, including chance event outcomes.
- **Support Vector Machines (SVM):** Find the hyperplane that best separates different classes in the feature spacc.
- **K-Nearest Neighbors (KNN):** Classifics data points based on the majority class of their nearest neighbors.
- **Neural Networks:** Composed of interconnected nodes (neurons) that process data in layers, capable of capturing complex patterns.

2. **Supervised, Unsupervised, and Reinforcement Learning**

Machine learning approaches are traditionally divided into three broad categories, each with distinct characteristics and applications:

a. Supervised Learning

Supervised learning involves training a model on a labeled dataset, where each input is paired with its correct output. The model learns to map inputs to outputs, making it suitable for tasks where historical data predicts future outcomes.

Characteristics:

- Requires labeled data.
- Aims to predict outcomes for new, unseen data.
- Common tasks include classification and regression.

Algorithms:

- Classification: Assigns input data into predefined categories.
- Examples: Spam detection, image recognition.
- Regression: Predicts a continuous value based on input data.
- Examples: House price prediction, sales forecasting.

Applications:

- Medical Diagnosis: Identifying diseases based on patient data.
- Email Filtering: Classifying emails as spam or not spam.
- Credit Scoring: Assessing the risk of loan applicants.

b. Unsupervised Learning

Unsupervised learning deals with unlabeled data, where the model seeks to identify underlying patterns or structures without predefined outcomes. This approach is useful for exploring data and finding hidden relationships.

Applications:

- Market Segmentation: Grouping customers based on purchasing behavior.
- Anomaly Detection: Identifying unusual patterns in data. Dimensionality Reduction: Simplifying data without losing essential information.

c. Reinforcement Learning

Reinforcement learning involves an agent that learns to make decisions by performing actions and receiving feedback in the form of rewards or penalties. The goal is to learn a strategy that maximizes cumulative rewards over time.

Characteristics:

- **SARSA (State-Action-Reward-State-Action):** Similar to Q-learning but updates values based on the next action taken.
- **Deep Q-Networks (DQN):** Combines Q-learning with deep neural networks to handle high-dimensional state spaces.

Applications:

- Robotics: Teaching robots to perform tasks through trial and error.
- Game Playing: Developing agents that can play games like chess or Go at a high level.
- Autonomous Vehicles: Enabling self-driving cars to navigate complex environments.

Comparison of Learning Types

ASPECT	SUPERVISED LEARNING	UNSUPERVISED LEARNING	REINFORCED LEARNING
Data Requirements	Requires Labeled data	Works with unlabeled data	No labeled data, learns from interaction with the environment
Learning Objectives	Learning a mapping from input to outpost	Discover underlying patterns or groupings	Learn a policy to maximize cumulative rewards
Common Algorithms	Linear Regression, Logistic Regression, SVM, Decision Trees, Neural Networks.	K-Means, Hierarchical Clustering, PCA, and Autoencoders.	Q-Learning, SARSA, Deep-Q Networks (DQN)
Applications	Medical diagnosis, email filtering, and credit scoring	Market segmentation, anomaly detection, and dimensionality reduction	Robotics, game playing, and autonomous vehicles

Understanding these learning paradigms is crucial for selecting the appropriate approach based on the problem at hand and the nature of the available data.

For more, visit: supervised learning vs unsupervised learning https://www.youtube.com/watch?v=1FZ0A1QCMWc

Chapter 4

Natural Language Processing

Natural Language Processing (NLP) is a pivotal component of Artificial Intelligence (AI) that enables machines to comprehend, interpret, and generate human language. In the business sector, NLP is transforming operations by enhancing customer interactions, streamlining processes, and extracting valuable insights from vast amounts of textual data. This chapter delves into the fundamental techniques of NLP and explores its primary applications in business: chatbots, machine translation, and sentiment analysis.

1. Techniques for Understanding and Generating Human Language

NLP employs various techniques to process and analyze human language, typically categorized into syntactic, semantic, and pragmatic approaches.

a. Syntactic Techniques

Syntactic analysis examines sentence structures to understand grammatical relationships between words. Key techniques include:

- **Tokenization:** Dividing text into individual words or tokens, facilitating discrete text processing.
- **Part-of-Speech (POS) Tagging:** Assigning grammatical tags (e.g., noun, verb, adjective) to each token, aiding in understanding word roles within sentences.
- **Parsing:** Analyzing sentence structures to construct parse trees that represent grammatical relationships among words.

b. Semantic Techniques

Semantic analysis focuses on understanding the meanings of words and sentences. Techniques include:

- **Named Entity Recognition (NER):** Identifying and classifying entities such as names of people, organizations, locations, and dates within text, crucial for information extraction tasks.

- **Word Embeddings:** Representing words in continuous vector spaces where semantically similar words are mapped to proximate points, enhancing machine understanding of word meanings.
- **Latent Semantic Analysis (LSA):** Analyzing relationships between documents and terms to uncover underlying concepts, assuming that words with similar meanings occur in similar contexts.
- **Semantic Parsing:** Converting natural language into machine-understandable representations, such as logical forms, to facilitate tasks like machine translation and question answering.

c. **Pragmatic Techniques**

Pragmatic analysis considers the context and intended use of language. Techniques include:

- **Coreference Resolution:** Determining which words or phrases refer to the same entity in a text, such as resolving pronouns to the nouns they refer to.
- **Discourse Analysis:** Understanding the structure and meaning of larger text units, such as paragraphs or entire documents, to capture the flow and coherence of ideas.

2. Applications in Chatbots, Machine Translation, and Sentiment Analysis

NLP techniques are integral to a range of business applications, including chatbots, machine translation, and sentiment analysis.

a. Chatbots

Chatbots are AI systems designed to simulate human conversation, enhancing customer service and engagement. NLP enables chatbots to understand and generate human language, facilitating tasks such as:

- **Intent Recognition:** Identifying the user's intention behind a query to provide appropriate responses.
- **Entity Recognition:** Extracting relevant information from user input, such as dates, locations, or product names.
- **Dialogue Management:** Maintaining context and managing the flow of conversation to ensure coherent and relevant interactions.
- **Response Generation:** Formulating appropriate and contextually relevant responses to user queries.

For instance, IBM's Watson Assistant utilizes NLP to handle customer inquiries, providing timely assistance and reducing wait times. (cio.com)

b. Machine Translation

Machine translation involves converting text or speech from one language to another, breaking down language barriers in global commerce. NLP techniques are essential for understanding the grammatical and semantic nuances of both source and target languages. Key components include:

- **Syntax and Grammar Analysis:** Understanding sentence structures to ensure accurate translation.
- **Word Sense Disambiguation:** Determining the correct meaning of words based on context to select the appropriate translation.
- **Alignment Models:** Mapping words and phrases between source and target languages to facilitate accurate translation.
- **Neural Machine Translation (NMT):** Utilizing deep learning models to improve translation quality by capturing complex language patterns.

NLP has revolutionized language translation, making global communication more accessible. Services like Google Translate employ NLP algorithms to provide real-time translations between multiple languages. (cio.com)

c. Sentiment Analysis

Sentiment analysis involves determining the emotional tone expressed in a piece of text, such as positive, negative, or neutral sentiments. NLP techniques enable machines to analyze vast amounts of text data to gauge public opinion, customer satisfaction, and market trends. Key methods include:

- **Text Preprocessing:** Cleaning and preparing text data by removing noise, such as stop words and punctuation.
- **Feature Extraction:** Identifying relevant features, such as n-grams or word embeddings, to represent the text.
- **Classification Algorithms:** Applying machine learning models, such as Support Vector Machines (SVMs) or Recurrent Neural Networks (RNNs), to classify sentiments.
- **Aspect-Based Sentiment Analysis:** Analyzing sentiments related to specific aspects or features within the text.

For example, companies use sentiment analysis to monitor brand reputation by analyzing social media posts and customer reviews. (cio.com)

Conclusion

Natural Language Processing is a fast-evolving field that links human language with machine understanding. By integrating syntactic, semantic, and pragmatic techniques, NLP enables machines to understand, interpret, and generate human language effectively. Its applications in chatbots, machine translation, and sentiment analysis have transformed many industries, enhancing user experiences and making communication more efficient. As NLP continues to improve, it promises even more advanced, context-aware language processing in the future.

Chapter 5
Computer Vision

Computer Vision (CV) is a multidisciplinary area within Artificial Intelligence (AI) that allows machines to interpret and analyze visual information like images and videos. In the business world, CV is transforming operations by improving customer experiences, streamlining processes, and offering valuable insights across many industries. This chapter reviews the key methods for helping machines understand visual data and looks at important applications in facial recognition, autonomous vehicles, and medical imaging.

1. Methods for Enabling Machines to Interpret Visual Data

To enable machines to interpret visual information, various techniques are used:

a. Image Preprocessing

Before analysis, images typically go through preprocessing to enhance quality and extract important features:

- **Normalization:** Adjusting pixel values to a standard range ensures consistency across images.
- **Noise Reduction:** Applying filters eliminates unwanted variations, enhancing image clarity.
- **Resizing and Scaling:** Standardizing image dimensions facilitates uniform processing.

b. Feature Extraction

Identifying and extracting meaningful features from images is essential for interpretation:

- **Edge Detection:** Techniques like the Sobel operator highlight boundaries in images, aiding object recognition.
- **Texture Analysis:** Methods such as Local Binary Patterns (LBP) analyze surface textures to differentiate between materials or objects.
- **Color Histograms:** Depicting the distribution of colors in an image helps with object identification and scene analysis.

c. Machine Learning and Deep Learning

Advanced algorithms allow machines to learn from data and get better with experience:

- **Supervised Learning:** Models trained on labeled datasets recognize patterns and predict outcomes. For example, Convolutional Neural Networks (CNNs) are widely used for image classification.
- **Unsupervised Learning:** Algorithms discover inherent structures in unlabeled data, useful for clustering similar images or spotting anomalies.
- **Reinforcement Learning:** Systems learn optimal behaviors by interacting with their environment and receiving feedback through rewards or penalties.

d. Object Detection and Recognition

Methods that allow machines to identify and locate objects within images:

- **Sliding Window:** A technique that moves a window across the image to detect objects at different positions and scales.
- **Region-Based CNNs (R-CNNs):** These models propose candidate regions in an image and classify them to improve detection accuracy.
- **YOLO (You Only Look Once):** A real-time object detection system that divides images into grids and predicts bounding boxes and class probabilities simultaneously.
- **Semantic Segmentation:** Assigning a class label to each pixel, useful in applications like medical imaging where precise structure delineation is necessary.

- **Instance Segmentation:** Differentiating between separate objects of the same class, allowing for the identification of multiple instances within an image.

2. **Applications in Facial Recognition, Autonomous Vehicles, and Medical Imaging**

Computer Vision has transformative applications across various industries:

a. **Facial Recognition**

Facial recognition systems identify and verify individuals based on facial features:

- **Feature Extraction:** Identifying key facial landmarks, such as eye distance or jawline shape.
- **Pattern Recognition:** Comparing extracted features against a database to find matches.

Applications

- **Security:** Strengthening access control in secure facilities by verifying authorized personnel.
- **Surveillance:** Monitoring public spaces to identify persons of interest.
- **Consumer Electronics:** Enabling user authentication on smartphones and other devices.

b. Autonomous Vehicles

Self-driving cars depend on Computer Vision to navigate and interpret their surroundings:

- **Object Detection:** Recognizing pedestrians, other vehicles, and obstacles to ensure safe travel.
- **Lane Detection:** Recognizing road markings to stay within lanes.
- **Traffic Sign Recognition:** Interpreting road signs to follow traffic laws.

Applications:

- **Navigation:** Allowing vehicles to plan routes and make driving decisions autonomously.
- **Safety:** Preventing accidents by detecting and responding to hazards in real time.
- **Mapping:** Creating detailed environment maps to support navigation and planning.

c. Medical Imaging

Computer Vision improves the analysis of medical images, supporting diagnosis and treatment planning:

- **Tumor Detection:** Identifying and isolating tumors in MRI and CT scans.

- **Organ Segmentation:** Accurately outlining organs to assess size, shape, and abnormalities.
- **Disease Progression Monitoring:** Comparing sequential images to evaluate disease progression or remission.

Applications:

- **Diagnostics:** Assisting radiologists in detecting conditions like cancers, fractures, and neurological disorders.
- **Surgical Planning:** Providing detailed anatomical information to prepare for surgical procedures.
- **Treatment Monitoring:** Tracking changes in medical images to evaluate treatment effectiveness.

Conclusion

Computer Vision is a vital field that enables machines to interpret and understand visual data, bridging the gap between human visual perception and machine analysis. Using advanced techniques in image preprocessing, feature extraction, and machine learning, machines can perform complex tasks such as facial recognition, autonomous navigation, and medical image analysis. As technology progresses, incorporating Computer Vision into different sectors continues to improve efficiency, safety, and service quality, showing its transformative effect on modern society.

Chapter 6
Robotics

Integrating Artificial Intelligence (AI) into robotic systems has significantly transformed business operations across various industries. This chapter explores how AI enhances robotic capabilities and examines its applications in manufacturing, healthcare, and service sectors.

1. Integration of AI in Robotic Systems

The fusion of AI and robotics has led to the development of intelligent systems capable of perception, decision-making, and learning. Key components of this integration include:

a. Perception

AI-equipped robots analyze sensory inputs, such as visual, auditory, and tactile data, to comprehend their environment. For instance, computer vision algorithms enable robots to identify objects, navigate spaces, and interact with humans. MIT researchers have developed an AI system that allows robots to learn self-control using vision alone, eliminating the need for additional sensors.

b. Decision-Making

AI algorithms, including machine learning and reinforcement learning, enable robots to make informed decisions based on sensory data and predefined objectives. This capability allows robots to adapt to new tasks and environments, enhancing their autonomy and efficiency. Google's DeepMind has developed AI models that boost robotic intelligence, allowing robots to perform complex tasks with greater reasoning and independence.

c. Learning and Adaptation

Machine learning techniques enable robots to learn from experience, improving their performance over time. This adaptability is essential for tasks that demand flexibility and the ability to manage diverse situations. The integration of large language models into robotic systems has accelerated progress in embodied AI, enabling robots to design and modify their own mechanisms.

2. Applications in Manufacturing, Healthcare, and Service Industries

The incorporation of AI into robotics has revolutionized various industries, enhancing efficiency, accuracy, and safety.

a. Manufacturing

In manufacturing, AI-driven robots are transforming production lines by completing complex tasks with accuracy and speed. They can adapt to schedule changes, optimize resource use, and maintain product quality through real-time monitoring and predictive maintenance. Collaborative robots (cobots) work alongside human workers, boosting productivity and safety. For example, Tesla has incorporated AI-powered robots into its Gigafactories, where robotic arms assemble cars with high precision, greatly improving manufacturing efficiency and quality.

b. Healthcare

In healthcare, AI-powered robots are revolutionizing patient care and diagnostics. Surgical robots, such as the da Vinci system, help surgeons perform minimally invasive procedures with greater precision, resulting in smaller incisions, quicker recovery times, and fewer complications. Service robots in hospitals are also experiencing double-digit annual growth, driven by automation in surgery, diagnostics, and patient support. Furthermore, AI-driven robots assist in managing large volumes of medical data, offering accurate diagnoses, recommending treatment plans, and monitoring patient progress, thereby enhancing the quality of care and patient outcomes.

c. Service Industries

In service industries, AI-powered robots improve customer experiences and operational efficiency. Robots are used in retail settings for tasks such as shelf management, interactive customer service, and automated checkout. In logistics and warehousing, AI-driven robots enhance inventory management, automate packing and picking, and enable real-time tracking, making last-mile delivery faster and safer. For example, Amazon has deployed robots in its warehouses to boost efficiency and lower employee injuries.

Conclusion

The integration of AI into robotic systems has led to significant advances across many industries, boosting efficiency, accuracy, and safety. In manufacturing, AI-powered robots improve production processes and work alongside human workers. In healthcare, AI-driven robots help with surgeries and patient care, leading to better outcomes and shorter recovery times. In service industries, AI robots improve customer service and make operations more efficient. As AI and robotics continue to evolve, their combined potential holds the promise of further innovations and improvements across many fields.

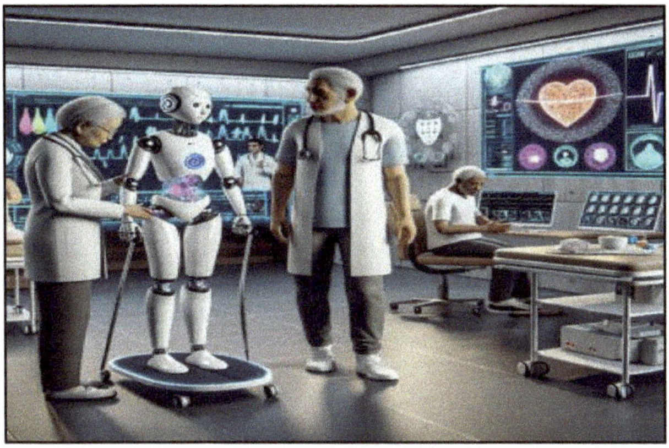

Chapter 7
Healthcare

Artificial Intelligence (AI) is revolutionizing the healthcare industry by enhancing diagnostics, personalizing treatments, and improving patient care. However, integrating AI into healthcare systems also presents significant ethical challenges. This chapter examines AI applications in healthcare and considers the ethical concerns they raise.

1. AI in Diagnostics, Personalized Medicine, and Patient Care

a. AI in Diagnostics

AI technologies, particularly machine learning and deep learning algorithms, are increasingly utilized to analyze complex medical data, enabling more accurate and timely diagnoses. Key applications include:

- **Medical Imaging Analysis:** AI algorithms assist in interpreting medical images, such as X-rays, MRIs, and CT scans, by detecting anomalies like tumors or fractures. For example, AI systems can identify early signs of diseases such as cancer, often with accuracy equal to or exceeding that of human radiologists. (forbes.com)
- **Predictive Analytics:** AI models examine patient data to forecast disease progression and outcomes. By recognizing patterns in large datasets, these models can predict the likelihood of conditions such as sepsis or heart failure, allowing for proactive treatment.
- **Genomic Data Interpretation:** AI supports the analysis of genomic sequences, helping identify genetic mutations linked to diseases. This is essential for understanding complex genetic disorders and creating targeted therapies.

b. Personalized Medicine

Personalized medicine tailors medical treatment to each patient's unique traits, including genetics, environment, and lifestyle. AI contributes to personalized medicine by:

- **Genomic Analysis:** AI algorithms analyze large amounts of genomic data to find genetic variations associated with diseases, supporting the creation of personalized treatment strategies.

- **Drug Discovery:** AI accelerates the drug discovery process by predicting how various compounds interact with targets and identifying potential candidates for clinical trials more effectively.
- **Treatment Optimization:** AI systems analyze patient data to recommend personalized treatment plans, improving effectiveness and reducing side effects.

c. **Patient Care**

AI enhances patient care by:

- **Virtual Health Assistants:** AI-powered chatbots and virtual assistants offer patients information about symptoms, medications, and treatment options, enhancing engagement and education.
- **Remote Monitoring:** AI algorithms analyze data from wearable devices to monitor chronic conditions, alerting healthcare providers to potential issues and enabling timely interventions.
- **Robotic Surgery:** AI-powered robotic systems support surgeons in executing precise, minimally invasive procedures, leading to shorter recovery times and better results.

2. Ethical Considerations and Challenges

The integration of AI into healthcare raises several ethical challenges that need to be addressed to protect patient safety, build trust, and promote fairness.

a. Bias and Fairness

AI systems can unintentionally reinforce biases in their training data, leading to unfair or discriminatory outcomes. For example, a study revealed that Black patients in the U.S. healthcare system received significantly lower 'risk scores' than white patients with similar medical conditions. This difference occurred because the algorithm used each patient's annual care costs as an indicator of their medical condition's complexity, unintentionally mirroring existing healthcare disparities. (cdc.gov)

To Mitigate Bias:

- **Diverse Data Collection:** Ensure training datasets are representative of diverse populations to prevent biased outcomes.
- **Bias Audits:** Regularly evaluate AI systems for biased decision-making and implement corrective measures as needed.

b. Transparency and Explainability

AI algorithms and deep learning models often operate as *"black boxes,"* making it difficult to understand how decisions are made. This lack of transparency can weaken trust and accountability in healthcare settings. Patients and healthcare providers may struggle to understand AI-generated recommendations, hindering informed decision-making.

To Enhance Transparency:

- **Explainable AI:** Create models that offer clear reasons for their outputs, helping clinicians and patients understand them.
- **Documentation:** Keep detailed records of AI system development, including data sources, model settings, and decision-making processes.

c. Data Privacy and Security

AI systems require access to large amounts of sensitive patient data, raising issues about privacy and security. Unauthorized access or data breaches can cause identity theft, discrimination, and loss of trust in healthcare institutions.

To Protect Data:

- **Data Encryption:** Use strong encryption methods to secure data during storage and transmission.

- **Access Controls:** Implement strict access protocols to ensure only authorized personnel can access sensitive information.
- **Informed Consent:** Clearly communicate to patients how their data will be used, ensuring they agree to its use in AI applications.

d. **Accountability and Liability**

Determining responsibility when AI systems make errors is complex. Questions arise about who should be held accountable for adverse outcomes: the developers, healthcare providers, or the AI system itself.

To Address Accountability:

- **Clear Guidelines:** Set policies outlining the roles and responsibilities of AI developers, healthcare providers, and institutions.
- **Liability Frameworks:** Create legal frameworks that establish liability in cases of AI-related errors, ensuring fair compensation for affected patients.

e. **Informed Consent**

Patients need to be fully informed about the role of AI in their diagnosis and treatment. However, the complexity of AI systems can make it hard to clearly communicate their functions and limitations.

To Improve Informed Consent:

- **Simplified Communication:** Use clear, non-technical language to explain AI applications to patients.
- **Educational Materials:** Provide resources to help patients understand how AI supports their care.

f. **Autonomy and Human Oversight**

While AI can improve decision-making, it should not replace human judgment. Maintaining human oversight ensures that ethical considerations and patient preferences are incorporated into care decisions.

To Preserve Autonomy:

- **Human-in-the-Loop Systems:** Design AI systems that support, rather than replace, healthcare providers' decisions.
- **Continuous Training:** Ensure healthcare professionals are trained to interpret and integrate AI recommendations appropriately.

g. **Equity and Access**

The deployment of AI in healthcare must consider equitable access to prevent the exacerbation of existing disparities. Unequal access to AI technologies can widen the gap between different socioeconomic groups.

To Promote Equity:

- **Inclusive Development:** Involve diverse stakeholders in the development of AI systems to address the needs of various populations.
- **Policy Interventions:** Implement policies that ensure equitable distribution of AI healthcare benefits.

Conclusion

AI has great potential to transform healthcare by improving diagnostics, personalizing treatments, and enhancing patient care. However, integrating AI requires careful consideration of ethical principles to protect patient safety, trust, and fairness. It is essential to address issues like bias, transparency, data privacy, accountability, informed consent, autonomy, and equity to ensure responsible and effective AI use in healthcare. By actively addressing these ethical challenges, stakeholders can maximize AI's benefits while upholding the core values of the medical profession.

Chapter 8
Artificial Intelligence in Finance

Artificial Intelligence (AI) is transforming the financial industry by enhancing algorithmic trading, strengthening fraud detection, and improving risk assessment methods. However, this integration also brings significant challenges and ethical issues that need careful consideration. This chapter explores AI applications in finance and their impact on financial markets and regulations.

1. AI in Finance: Algorithmic Trading, Fraud Detection, and Risk Evaluation

a. Algorithmic Trading

Algorithmic trading employs computer algorithms to execute trading strategies rapidly and in large volumes, surpassing human capabilities. AI enhances algorithmic trading by:

- **Data Analysis:** AI algorithms analyze vast amounts of market data to identify patterns and trends, supporting more informed trading decisions.
- **Predictive Modeling:** Machine learning models forecast market movements, aiding in the development of strategies that adapt to market changes.
- **Execution Optimization:** AI improves trade execution by determining optimal times and methods for entering or exiting trades, reducing market impact and costs.

Example: Quantitative hedge funds leverage AI-driven algorithms to analyze market data and execute trades, aiming to profit from short-term market inefficiencies.

b. Fraud Detection

AI plays a crucial role in identifying and preventing fraudulent activities in the financial sector:

- **Anomaly Detection:** Machine learning models detect unusual patterns in transaction data that could indicate fraud.
- **Real-Time Monitoring:** AI systems oversee transactions in real time, enabling immediate responses to potential fraudulent activities.
- **Behavioral Analysis:** AI examines customer behavior to identify deviations from normal patterns, flagging possible fraudulent actions.

Example: Banks utilize AI to monitor transactions for signs of fraud, such as unusual spending or sudden changes in account activity.

c. Risk Assessment

AI Enhances Risk Assessment By:

- **Credit Scoring:** Machine learning models evaluate creditworthiness using a broad range of data, including unconventional sources like social media activity.
- **Market Risk Analysis:** AI assesses market risks by analyzing economic indicators, market sentiment, and other relevant data.
- **Operational Risk Management:** AI identifies and mitigates operational risks by analyzing internal processes and external factors that might threaten financial stability.

Example: Financial institutions use AI to assess the credit risk of loan applicants by reviewing their financial history and other relevant data.

2. Impact on Financial Markets and Regulations

The integration of AI into finance has profound implications for markets and regulatory frameworks:

a. Market Efficiency and Liquidity

AI Contributes to Market Efficiency By:

- **Improving Price Discovery:** AI algorithms process extensive data to provide more accurate pricing information.
- **Boosting Liquidity:** AI-driven trading strategies can increase market liquidity by enabling faster and more efficient trades.

Example: High-frequency trading firms use AI to execute large volumes of orders quickly, thereby enhancing market liquidity.

b. Systemic Risks and Market Stability

While AI Offers Benefits, it also Introduces Potential Risks:

- **Herding Behavior:** Widespread use of similar AI models can lead to herding, where many market participants make identical decisions simultaneously, potentially heightening volatility.
- **Flash Crashes:** AI-based trading algorithms may, under certain conditions, contribute to rapid market crashes.

Example: In 2010, the U.S. stock market experienced a "flash crash" in which major indices plummeted within minutes, partly due to algorithmic trading.

c. Regulatory Challenges

AI's Role in Finance Raises Several Regulatory Issues:

- **Model Transparency:** The complexity of AI models can make it challenging for regulators to comprehend and evaluate their decision-making processes.
- **Data Privacy:** The extensive use of personal and financial data in AI models raises concerns about privacy and security.
- **Bias and Fairness:** AI models might unintentionally reinforce biases from their training data, leading to unfair or discriminatory outcomes.

Example: The U.S. Securities and Exchange Commission (SEC) has expressed concerns about AI's potential to cause market instability and has called for greater oversight of AI in financial markets. (reuters.com)

d. Regulatory Responses

Regulators are actively addressing AI-related challenges in finance:

- **Creating Frameworks:** Agencies are developing guidelines and frameworks to promote the responsible use of AI in financial services.
- **Increasing Oversight:** Regulators are strengthening supervision of AI applications to manage risks and safeguard market stability.

- **Promoting Transparency:** Efforts are underway to improve transparency regarding AI models used in financial decision-making.

Example: The Organization for Economic Co-operation and Development (OECD) has issued guidelines on AI use in finance, emphasizing transparency, fairness, and responsibility. (axios.com)

Conclusion

AI is transforming the financial industry, leading to major improvements in algorithmic trading, fraud detection, and risk analysis. However, its adoption also brings challenges related to market stability, regulation, and ethics. A balanced approach that leverages AI's benefits while effectively managing its risks is essential for sustainable growth in finance. Continuous collaboration among financial institutions, regulators, and technology developers is vital to ensuring AI's positive impact on the economic ecosystem.

Chapter 9

Artificial Intelligence in Education

Artificial Intelligence (AI) is revolutionizing the educational sector by enabling personalized learning experiences and developing intelligent tutoring systems. These innovations aim to meet individual learning needs, enhance engagement, and improve academic outcomes. However, implementing AI in education also introduces challenges, particularly concerning equity and access. This chapter discusses the integration of AI in education, focusing on personalized learning and intelligent tutoring systems, and explores the related challenges and ethical issues from a business perspective.

1. Personalized Learning Experiences and Intelligent Tutoring Systems

a. Personalized Learning Experiences

Personalized learning involves educational methods that adapt instruction to fit each student's learning style, pace, and preferences. AI supports personalized learning through several methods:

- **Adaptive Learning Platforms:** These platforms use machine learning algorithms to analyze student performance data, adjusting content difficulty and pace to meet each learner's needs. By continuously tracking progress, adaptive systems offer customized learning paths, ensuring students face appropriate challenges and receive the support they need.
- **Predictive Analytics:** AI-based predictive models evaluate various data points, such as past performance, engagement levels, and behavioral patterns, to forecast future learning outcomes. This allows educators to intervene early and provide targeted assistance to students at risk.
- **Real-Time Feedback:** AI tools can give instant, constructive feedback on assignments and assessments, helping students recognize mistakes and learn from them quickly. This prompt feedback encourages a growth mindset and ongoing improvement.

b. **Intelligent Tutoring Systems (ITS)**

Intelligent Tutoring Systems are AI-enabled platforms designed to deliver personalized teaching and feedback, mimicking one-on-one tutoring. Key features of ITS include:

- **Natural Language Processing (NLP):** Advanced NLP techniques enable ITS to comprehend and respond to student inputs in natural language, creating interactive and engaging learning experiences. For example, Auto Tutor uses NLP to hold conversations with students, adjusting responses based on interactions.
- **Cognitive Modeling:** ITS often includes cognitive models, such as Bayesian Knowledge Tracing, to monitor and predict student learning progress. These models assess a student's likelihood of mastering a concept, enabling the system to adapt instruction accordingly.
- **Adaptive Problem Generation:** Based on real-time assessments of understanding, ITS can generate problems or exercises suited to the learner's current level, helping them master concepts before moving on to more difficult material.

c. **Benefits of AI in Personalized Learning and ITS**

The use of AI in Education Offers Several Benefits:

- **Increased Engagement:** Custom learning experiences that align with students' interests and learning styles boost motivation and participation.
- **Better Learning Results:** Personalized instruction addresses specific gaps, improving comprehension and retention.
- **Scalability:** AI-driven systems can provide personalized teaching to many students at once, making quality education more accessible.

2. **Challenges in Implementation and Equity**

Despite the promising potential of AI in education, several obstacles must be addressed to ensure effective use and fair access:

a. **Data Privacy and Security**

Gathering and analyzing large amounts of student data raises privacy concerns. Protecting this data is critical to maintaining trust and complying with laws such as the Family Educational Rights and Privacy Act (FERPA).

b. **Algorithmic Bias**

AI systems can inherit biases from their training data, leading to unfair or discriminatory outcomes. For example, if an ITS is trained chiefly on data from a particular demographic, it may not perform equally well for students outside that group, potentially widening existing educational gaps.

c. Digital Divide

Access to AI-based educational tools often depends on reliable internet and modern devices. Students from low-income families or rural areas may lack these resources, creating inequalities in learning opportunities.

d. Teacher Training and Acceptance

Teachers need proper training to incorporate AI tools into their teaching effectively. Resistance from educators can slow down or hinder AI's integration into classrooms.

c. Ethical Considerations

Using AI in education raises questions about automation levels, the role of human teachers, and the risk of AI replacing human interaction, which is vital for social and emotional growth.

f. Equity in AI Deployment

Ensuring AI technology is distributed fairly is essential to preventing the widening of achievement gaps. This involves providing equal access to AI tools, addressing algorithmic bias, and ensuring AI applications are culturally and contextually appropriate for diverse student populations.

Conclusion

Artificial Intelligence can revolutionize education by enabling personalized learning experiences and intelligent tutoring systems tailored to each individual's needs. While these advancements offer significant benefits, it is essential to address challenges such as data privacy, algorithm bias, digital inequality, and ethical concerns. By actively tackling these issues, stakeholders can maximize AI's potential in education and ensure all students have access to high-quality, personalized learning opportunities.

Chapter 10

Artificial Intelligence in Entertainment

Artificial Intelligence (AI) is revolutionizing the entertainment industry by transforming content creation, distribution, and consumption. From personalized recommendation systems to innovative content creation tools and immersive gaming experiences, AI's influence is pervasive. This chapter examines the integration of AI in entertainment, focusing on personalized learning and intelligent tutoring systems, and explores the associated challenges and ethical considerations from a business perspective.

1. AI in Entertainment: Recommendation Systems, Content Creation, and Gaming

a. Recommendation Systems

Recommendation systems are crucial for guiding consumers to content that aligns with their preferences, thereby enhancing user engagement and satisfaction. AI-powered recommendation engines analyze extensive datasets, including viewing history, ratings, and demographic information, to deliver personalized content suggestions.

Streaming Platforms: Services like Netflix and Spotify utilize AI algorithms to curate personalized playlists and movie recommendations. By analyzing user behavior and preferences, these platforms suggest content that users are likely to enjoy, increasing engagement and retention.

E-commerce and Retail: Online retailers employ AI to recommend products based on browsing history and purchase patterns, improving the shopping experience and boosting sales.

b. Content Creation

AI is transforming content creation by automating various production tasks, allowing creators to focus on more strategic and creative endeavors.

- **Music Production:** AI tools assist in composing music, generating melodies, and even producing entire tracks. For instance, AI-generated music accounted for 20% of new releases on streaming platforms, signaling a significant shift in music production dynamics.
- **Video Editing and Post-Production:** AI algorithms streamline tasks such as video editing, color correction, and special effects, reducing production time and costs. This enhances efficiency, enabling faster content delivery and more engaging storytelling.
- **Scriptwriting and Story Development:** AI examines audience data and existing scripts to suggest plotlines, dialogues, and character arcs, supporting writers in creating compelling stories.

c. **Gaming**

In the gaming industry, AI enhances gameplay by creating more dynamic and responsive environments.

- **Non-Player Characters (NPCs):** AI-powered NPCs exhibit realistic behaviors and adapt to player actions, offering a more immersive gaming experience. Approximately 70% of gamers prefer AI-driven NPCs for more realistic interactions.
- **Procedural Content Generation:** AI algorithms generate game levels, environments, and scenarios, providing unique

experiences in each playthrough and increasing the game's replayability.

- **Adaptive Difficulty:** AI adjusts game difficulty in real-time based on player performance, ensuring a balanced and engaging challenge.

2. **Influence on Consumer Behavior and Industry Trends**

AI's integration into entertainment has significantly impacted consumer behavior and industry trends.

a. **Improved Personalization**

Consumers now expect tailored experiences, and AI delivers by analyzing individual preferences and behaviors to customize content and interactions.

- **Streaming Services:** Platforms like Netflix and Spotify use AI to recommend content, resulting in higher user engagement and satisfaction. AI-driven personalized playlists boost user retention by 35%.
- **E-commerce:** Online retailers utilize AI to suggest products, enhancing the shopping experience and increasing sales.

b. **Data-Informed Decision Making**

AI enables entertainment companies to make smarter decisions based on data analysis.

- **Content Development:** By studying audience preferences and trends, AI helps create content that appeals to target audiences, increasing chances of success.
- **Marketing Tactics:** AI-based analytics assist in designing targeted marketing campaigns, optimizing advertising budgets, and improving conversion rates.

c. **Improved Operational Efficiency**

AI Simplifies Operations within the Entertainment Industry.

- **Automated Content Moderation:** AI algorithms identify and filter inappropriate content, ensuring compliance with regulations and community standards.
- **Customer Support:** AI-powered chatbots manage customer inquiries, offering prompt responses and allowing human agents to focus on more complex issues.

d. **Ethical Issues and Challenges**

The use of AI in Entertainment Raises Various Ethical Concerns.

- **Data Privacy:** Collecting and analyzing large amounts of personal data for AI-driven recommendations creates privacy risks. Protecting data and maintaining transparency are essential.
- **Job Losses:** Automation of tasks traditionally performed by humans, such as content moderation and customer support, may lead to job cuts, requiring reskilling and adaptation.

- **Bias and Fairness:** AI systems can unintentionally reinforce biases present in their training data, resulting in unfair or discriminatory outcomes. Constant monitoring and adjustments are necessary to reduce these biases.

e. **Market Growth and Economic Impact**

The integration of AI is Driving Significant Growth in the Entertainment Industry.

- **Industry Revenue:** The global entertainment and media sector is projected to reach $3.5 trillion in revenue by 2029, driven largely by the increasing use of AI-powered advertising. (reuters.com)
- **Investment in AI:** Many entertainment companies plan to boost their AI investments, showing a strong belief in AI's ability to foster growth and innovation.

Conclusion

Artificial intelligence is transforming the entertainment industry by improving personalization, simplifying content creation, and enhancing gaming experiences. Its impact also influences consumer behavior, raising expectations for customized content and data-driven interactions. While AI offers many advantages, it also brings challenges related to ethics, privacy, and jobs. Addressing these issues responsibly through thoughtful AI development and use will be crucial for the sustainable growth of the entertainment sector.

Chapter 11

Ethical Considerations in Artificial Intelligence

Artificial Intelligence (AI) has become a cornerstone of modern business operations, influencing sectors such as healthcare, finance, education, and entertainment. As AI systems increasingly drive decisions that impact human lives, ethical considerations, including bias, transparency, accountability, fairness, and discrimination, have gained prominence. This chapter explores these ethical challenges, examining their implications and strategies for businesses to address them effectively.

1. **Bias, Transparency, and Accountability in AI Systems**

a. **Bias in AI Systems**

Bias in AI refers to systematic, unfair discrimination that can occur when AI systems produce prejudiced results due to incorrect assumptions in the machine learning process. This bias can manifest in various forms:

- **Data Bias:** If the training data is unrepresentative or contains historical prejudices, the AI system may perpetuate these biases. For example, an AI recruitment tool trained on data from a predominantly male workforce might favor male candidates, unintentionally discriminating against women.
- **Algorithmic Bias:** Even with unbiased data, the design of the algorithm can introduce bias. This can occur if the algorithm's parameters or decision-making steps are not carefully adjusted to prevent favoring certain groups over others.
- **Feedback Loops:** AI systems can reinforce existing biases by learning from their own outputs. For instance, a biased recommendation system might suggest content that aligns with existing prejudices, further entrenching those biases.

b. **Transparency in AI Systems**

Transparency in AI involves making the operations and decisions of AI systems understandable to users and stakeholders. Transparent AI systems enable:

- **Interpretability:** Users can understand how and why decisions are made, fostering trust and supporting informed decision-making.

- **Auditability:** Transparent systems can be reviewed and audited to identify and fix biases, ensuring compliance with ethical standards and regulations.
- **Explainability:** Providing clear explanations for AI-driven decisions helps stakeholders understand the reasoning behind outcomes, which is especially important in sectors like healthcare and criminal justice.

c. **Accountability in AI Systems**

Accountability in AI means the responsibility of individuals or organizations for the results produced by AI systems. Building accountability includes:

- **Clear Ownership:** Identifying who is responsible for the development, deployment, and oversight of AI systems.
- Redress Mechanisms: Implementing processes to address and rectify adverse outcomes or harms caused by AI decisions.
- **Ethical Governance:** Developing frameworks and policies that guide the ethical use of AI, ensuring systems align with societal values and norms.

2. Ensuring Fairness and Reducing Discrimination in AI Systems

a. Ensuring Fairness in AI Systems

Fairness in AI aims to prevent systems from producing discriminatory outcomes against individuals or groups. Achieving fairness involves:

- **Bias Detection and Reduction:** Regularly auditing AI systems to identify and fix biases in data and algorithms. Techniques such as fairness-enhancing interventions can be used to adjust models and data to promote equitable results.
- **Inclusive Data Gathering:** Ensuring training data represents diverse populations to avoid reinforcing existing societal biases.
- **Stakeholder Participation:** Involving diverse groups in developing and evaluating AI systems to include multiple perspectives and identify potential biases.

b. Reducing Discrimination in AI Systems

Discrimination occurs when AI systems produce outcomes that unfairly disadvantage certain groups. Reducing discrimination includes:

- **Algorithmic Fairness Checks:** Performing thorough evaluations of AI systems to assess how they impact different demographics and ensure fair treatment.
- **Legal Compliance:** Following laws and regulations that prohibit discrimination, such as the Equal Credit Opportunity Act, which requires that credit decisions be made without regard to race, color, religion, sex, or national origin.
- **Ongoing Monitoring:** Continuously monitoring and evaluating AI systems to identify and correct discriminatory patterns over time.

Conclusion

As AI becomes more integrated into business operations, addressing ethical issues related to bias, transparency, accountability, fairness, and discrimination is essential. By proactively tackling these challenges, organizations can develop AI systems that are ethical, trustworthy, and aligned with societal values, ensuring AI serves the collective good without reinforcing existing inequalities.

Chapter 12

The Future of Work in the Age of Artificial Intelligence

Artificial Intelligence (AI) is rapidly transforming the global workforce, presenting both opportunities and challenges for businesses. As AI technologies advance, they are reshaping employment landscapes, automating certain tasks while creating new roles in emerging sectors. This chapter examines AI's impact on employment from a business perspective, explores strategies for workforce adaptation, and emphasizes the importance of reskilling to navigate the evolving job market.

1. **Impact of AI on Employment and Job Displacement**
a. **Job Displacement Due to AI**

The integration of AI across industries has led to significant shifts in employment patterns. Repetitive, routine tasks are increasingly being automated, leading to job losses in certain areas. Key sectors affected include:

- **Manufacturing and Production:** Automation has enhanced processes, reducing the need for manual labor in assembly lines and factories. Robots and AI systems can perform tasks more efficiently and precisely than humans, decreasing demand for certain manufacturing roles.
- **Customer Service:** AI-driven chatbots and virtual assistants are managing customer inquiries, complaints, and support requests, reducing the need for human customer service representatives. This change is especially noticeable in sectors like retail and telecommunications.
- **Transportation and Logistics:** Autonomous vehicles and drones are transforming the transportation and logistics sectors. Self-driving trucks and delivery drones are likely to replace human drivers and couriers, potentially displacing many jobs.
- **Administrative and Clerical Work:** AI tools are automating tasks such as data entry, scheduling, and document

management, lowering the demand for administrative assistants and clerks.

b. **Economic Implications of Job Displacement**

The displacement of workers due to AI raises several economic concerns:

- **Unemployment Rates:** While the creation of new roles might balance AI-driven job losses, there is a risk of higher unemployment in the short term. Displaced workers may struggle to find new employment, especially if they lack the skills for emerging job sectors.
- **Wage Inequality:** The rising demand for high-skilled workers familiar with AI and related technologies could lead to wage gaps. Conversely, workers in roles vulnerable to automation might see their wages stagnate or decline as demand for their skills decreases.
- **Economic Inequality:** Displaced workers, particularly those in low-wage, low-skill jobs, may find it difficult to secure new opportunities, worsening economic inequality. This group tends to be more vulnerable to the negative impacts of technological disruption.

c. **Job Creation and Transformation**

Despite concerns about job displacement, AI also fosters job creation and transformation:

- **Emerging Roles:** New career paths are developing in areas like AI development, data science, machine learning engineering, and cybersecurity. These positions require specialized skills and provide opportunities for workers to shift into growing industries.
- **Job Augmentation:** Often, AI is used to enhance human abilities rather than replace them. For instance, AI tools can help healthcare professionals diagnose diseases more accurately and quickly.
- **Productivity Gains:** Automation driven by AI can boost productivity, potentially spurring economic growth and leading to the emergence of new industries and job opportunities.

2. **Strategies for Workforce Adaptation and Reskilling**

To address the challenges of AI-related job displacement, businesses need to adopt strategies that support workforce adaptation and reskilling:

a. **Lifelong Learning and Continuous Education**

- **Upskilling and Reskilling Programs:** Employees should pursue ongoing education to develop skills relevant to the changing job landscape. This includes training in AI technologies, data analysis, and other sought-after skills.
- **Online Education Platforms:** The widespread availability of online courses and certifications offers accessible ways for

workers to improve their skills. Platforms like Coursera, edX, and Udacity offer programs tailored to different industries and skill levels.

- **Corporate Training Initiatives:** Employers can support their employees through training programs that prepare them for new technological demands. This benefits both staff and organizations by creating a more flexible and skilled workforce.

b. Policy Interventions and Government Initiatives

- **Social Safety Nets:** Governments can introduce policies such as unemployment benefits, job placement services, and financial aid to assist workers during transition periods caused by AI-driven displacement.
- **Public-Private Partnerships:** Collaborations among government, educational institutions, and private companies can help develop targeted training programs and resources aligned with labor market needs.
- **Investment in Education:** Increasing funding for education systems that focus on STEM (Science, Technology, Engineering, and Mathematics) and digital literacy will better prepare future generations for an AI-centered economy.

c. Fostering Adaptability and Resilience

- **Soft Skills Development:** In addition to technical skills, developing soft skills such as critical thinking, creativity, emotional intelligence, and adaptability is crucial. These skills are less prone to automation and will continue to provide value in the workforce.

- **Career Counseling and Guidance:** Offering workers access to career counseling services can help them identify transferable skills and explore new career paths that match their interests and the changing job market.
- **Entrepreneurship Support:** Promoting and supporting entrepreneurship can lead to the creation of new businesses and employment opportunities. Providing resources, mentorship, and access to funding can empower individuals to start their own ventures.

d. Ethical Considerations and Inclusivity

- **Equity in Reskilling Opportunities:** Ensuring that reskilling programs are accessible to all workers, regardless of socioeconomic background, is vital to prevent widening existing inequalities.
- **Inclusive Policy Development:** Policymakers should consider the diverse needs of the workforce when designing programs and initiatives, ensuring that marginalized and vulnerable groups are not left behind in the transition to an AI-driven economy.
- **Ethical AI Deployment:** Organizations should follow ethical guidelines for AI implementation, considering the social and economic impacts on workers and communities. This includes

transparency in decision-making processes and accountability for the outcomes of AI deployment.

Conclusion

The integration of AI into the workforce presents a complex landscape of challenges and opportunities for businesses. While AI has the potential to displace specific jobs, it also offers avenues for job creation and transformation. By implementing comprehensive strategies focused on lifelong learning, policy support, adaptability, and inclusivity, organizations can navigate the evolving employment landscape. Proactive efforts in reskilling and workforce adaptation are essential to ensure that the benefits of AI are widely shared and that workers are prepared to thrive in the future of work.

Chapter 13

Privacy and Security in the Age of Artificial Intelligence

Artificial Intelligence (AI) is revolutionizing business operations, offering unparalleled opportunities for innovation and efficiency. However, this rapid advancement also introduces significant challenges related to data privacy and cybersecurity. As AI systems increasingly process vast amounts of sensitive information, implementing robust privacy protections and security measures becomes imperative. This chapter examines the privacy and cybersecurity risks associated with AI from a business perspective, reviews existing regulations, and highlights best practices for addressing these challenges.

1. Data Privacy Concerns and Cybersecurity Risks

a. Data Privacy Concerns

Data privacy involves the proper management, processing, storage, and sharing of personal information. In the context of AI, several privacy issues have emerged:

- **Informed Consent:** AI systems often require access to extensive datasets, including personal and sensitive data. Ensuring individuals are aware of how their data will be used and obtaining their explicit consent is crucial.
- **Data Minimization:** AI models can unintentionally collect more information than necessary for their purpose, leading to overreach and potential privacy breaches.
- **Anonymization and Re-identification:** Even when data is anonymized, advanced AI techniques can sometimes re-identify individuals, posing privacy risks.
- **Data Sharing and Third-Party Access:** Sharing data with third parties, such as AI service providers, raises concerns about the control and security of personal information.

b. Cybersecurity Risks

Cybersecurity focuses on protecting systems, networks, and data from digital attacks, unauthorized access, and harm. AI introduces various cybersecurity threats:

- **Adversarial Attacks:** AI systems can be targeted by inputs designed to deceive or mislead them, causing incorrect outputs or system failures.
- **Model Inversion:** Attackers may extract sensitive information from AI models, including training data, by analyzing model outputs.
- **Data Poisoning:** Malicious actors can corrupt AI training datasets with false data, compromising the model's accuracy and trustworthiness.
- **Insider Threats:** Trusted employees or individuals with access to AI systems might intentionally or unintentionally cause damage, leading to data breaches or disruptions.

2. Regulatory Frameworks and Best Practices

a. Regulatory Frameworks

To address the privacy and security challenges posed by AI, various regulatory frameworks have been established:

- **General Data Protection Regulation (GDPR):** Implemented by the European Union, GDPR establishes strict guidelines for data protection, focusing on transparency, accountability, and individuals' rights regarding their personal data.
- **California Consumer Privacy Act (CCPA):** This U.S. state law grants California resident's rights to access, delete, and opt out of the sale of their personal data, strengthening consumer privacy protections.

- **Health Insurance Portability and Accountability Act (HIPAA):** In the U.S., HIPAA sets standards for protecting health information, including provisions relevant to AI applications in healthcare.
- **New York Department of Financial Services (DFS) Guidance:** In October 2024, the DFS released guidance for financial institutions on reducing cybersecurity risks related to AI, highlighting the importance of updated risk assessments and effective response plans.

b. Best Practices

Organizations can adopt several best practices to enhance data privacy and cybersecurity in AI systems:

- **Data Encryption:** Applying strong encryption protocols for data at rest and in transit ensures that unauthorized individuals cannot access sensitive information.
- **Access Controls:** Implementing strict access controls and authentication methods, such as multi-factor authentication (MFA), limits data access to authorized personnel only.
- **Regular Audits and Monitoring:** Performing regular security audits and ongoing monitoring helps detect vulnerabilities and potential threats in AI systems.
- **Employee Training:** Educating employees about data privacy principles, cybersecurity threats, and safe practices reduces human error risks that could lead to security breaches.

- **Data Minimization:** Collecting only the data necessary for the specific AI purpose minimizes privacy risks.
- **Third-Party Risk Management:** Evaluating and managing the security measures of third-party vendors involved in AI development or deployment ensures they meet the organization's privacy and security standards.

Conclusion

As AI continues to influence various areas of business, addressing data privacy and cybersecurity concerns remains crucial. By adhering to established regulations and adopting robust best practices, organizations can mitigate risks and foster trust with consumers and stakeholders. Continuous vigilance, adapting to emerging threats, and a commitment to ethical AI development are vital to protecting privacy and security in the digital age.

Chapter 14
The Future Of Artificial Intelligence

Artificial Intelligence (AI) is rapidly transforming business landscapes, offering unprecedented opportunities for innovation and efficiency. This chapter explores emerging AI technologies and research areas, highlighting potential breakthroughs and their implications for businesses.

1. **Emerging Technologies and Research Areas in AI**

a. **Human-AI Interaction**

Advancements in human-AI interaction are focusing on developing AI systems that are transparent, explainable, and ethically responsible. Enhancing usability and building trust are key objectives that enable more effective collaboration between humans and AI systems. For instance, the development of AI agents capable of independent reasoning and decision-making, such as Manus by Butterfly Effect Technology, demonstrates significant progress in this area.

b. AI Safety and Alignment

AI safety is an interdisciplinary field dedicated to preventing accidents, misuse, or harmful outcomes from AI. It encompasses AI alignment, ensuring AI systems act as intended, as well as risk monitoring and increased robustness. The establishment of AI Safety Institutes, such as those in the UK and the US, underscores the importance of this field in promoting safe AI development.

c. Organoid Intelligence

Organoid intelligence leverages 3D cultures of human brain cells (brain organoids) and brain-machine interface technologies to create biohybrid systems. These systems may offer faster, more efficient, and more powerful computing capabilities than traditional silicon-based systems, potentially requiring only a fraction of the energy. While still in early stages, this field holds promise for revolutionizing computing and AI applications.

d. AI-Augmented Design and Creativity

AI-augmented design combines human creativity with computational power, enabling new levels of innovation in fields like architecture, fashion, and graphic design. AI's ability to analyze and learn from large datasets allows it to identify patterns and suggest design options that may not be obvious to human designers, thereby enhancing the creative process.

e. AI for Environmental Sustainability

AI's potential to support environmental sustainability is extensive. It can optimize energy consumption in large-scale systems through data collection and deep learning, improve weather predictions, and monitor wildlife and ecosystems with unprecedented precision. In agriculture, AI-driven technologies can forecast crop yields, monitor soil conditions, and optimize resource use (water, fertilizers) to boost productivity while minimizing environmental impact.

2. Potential Breakthroughs and Their Implications

a. Quantum-Enhanced AI Algorithms

The integration of quantum computing and AI has enabled quantum-enhanced AI algorithms to solve optimization problems that were once computationally intractable. These advances have significant implications across fields such as drug discovery, materials science, financial modeling, and logistics, enabling faster, more efficient solutions to complex challenges.

b. AI-Driven Innovations in Healthcare

AI-powered tools are enabling early disease detection, personalized treatments, and drug discovery. By analyzing large amounts of medical data, AI algorithms can identify patterns and insights that human experts might miss, leading to more accurate diagnoses and targeted therapies. This advancement has the potential to transform healthcare delivery and improve patient outcomes.

c. Autonomous Vehicles and Robotics

Progress in AI is advancing the development of autonomous vehicles and robots that can navigate complex environments and interact intelligently with their surroundings. This technology promises to revolutionize transportation, logistics, and manufacturing industries by increasing efficiency and safety. Companies like Tesla, Waymo, and Uber are improving navigation algorithms and integrating AI-powered sensors to enhance vehicle safety and efficiency.

d. Conversational AI and Natural Language Processing (NLP)

Advances in NLP are making AI chatbots and virtual assistants more human-like in their interactions. Breakthroughs in language understanding and generation will enable more natural and effective communication between humans and machines, enhancing user experience across various applications. The development of AI agents capable of independent reasoning and decision-making, such as Manus by Butterfly Effect Technology, demonstrates significant progress in this area. (en.wikipedia.org)

e. AI in Space Observation and Data Technology

AI is revolutionizing space observation and data technology by enabling real-time detection, data analysis, and image enhancement. This transforms how celestial events and anomalies are identified, enabling scientists to automate data-intensive tasks and focus on strategic research. The Genesis Mission, launched by the United States federal government, aims to accelerate scientific research through advanced AI technologies, including applications in space exploration.

Conclusion

Artificial Intelligence is experiencing rapid growth across many areas, from human-AI interaction and AI safety to quantum algorithms and applications in healthcare and space exploration. These new technologies and research fields are set to reshape industries, expand human capabilities, and address complex global issues. As AI continues to develop, it's crucial for businesses to consider the ethical, societal, and economic impacts of these advances to ensure their benefits are shared responsibly and fairly.

Anthony O'Brien

Executive Bio

Tony O'Brien is Managing Partner and Chief Strategy Officer at Fyntra AI, a nationally recognized provider of enterprise AI solutions. With more than 30 years of senior leadership experience, Tony combines domain expertise in energy, real estate, and equities with a proven track record of building high-performing sales organizations and commercializing complex products.

Career Highlights And Impact

- **Commercial Leadership:** Recruited, trained, and scaled a 400-person sales force across 13 deregulated states while launching Glacial Energy, driving monthly revenues to $30 million.
- **Entrepreneurial Success:** Founded and ran Spinnaker Partners, a proprietary hedge fund, for 19 years and later

established RealEstateLender.com, which grew to become a top-10 commercial lender.

- **Market Entry And Scaling:** As Managing Director of SFE/FE Energy (Summitt Energy subsidiary), led go-to-market efforts to position energy brands in the Commercial & Industrial segment and built a responsive, results-driven sales organization.
- **Cross-Sector Expertise:** Deep experience in B2B sales, marketing, AI strategy, and team development, helping organizations translate advanced technology into measurable revenue and operational gains.
- **Leadership Style And Value Proposition:** Tony is a strategic operator who focuses on measurable outcomes: building scalable revenue engines, aligning product strategy with market needs, and institutionalizing sales and operational processes. His background gives clients and partners confidence in navigating regulated markets, complex channel builds, and AI commercialization.

Publications

Author - *"Comprehensive Guide to Private Money Markets"* (2021 – Best Seller).

Author – *"Build an AI Ready Business"* (2026)

Tony combines entrepreneurial rigor with enterprise execution to accelerate growth and operationalize AI across regulated and data-intensive industries.

www.ingramcontent.com/pod-product-compliance
Lightning Source LLC
LaVergne TN
LVHW050937210926
848482LV00013B/640
* 9 7 9 8 2 9 5 5 8 9 6 9 0 *